Guiding Teens through a Social Media-Driven World

Table of Contents

We don't have a choice on whether we do social
media, the question is how well we do it.

Chapter 1. Introduction

In the Special Report titled 'Guiding Teens through a Social Media-Driven World', we delve into the dynamic interaction between today's teenagers and the ubiquitous realm of social media. The world is more connected than ever before, and nowhere is this more evident than in our digitally-driven youth. Navigating this new landscape can often seem daunting for both teens and parents alike. But fret not! This report, bursting with engaging insights and backed by comprehensive research, aims to turn those concerns into confidence. It offers a practical roadmap to help your teen harness the power of social media responsibly while minimizing its pitfalls. Experience the thrill of understanding, guiding, and effectively connecting with your teens in their digital space. Illuminate the shadowy corners of social media and transform them into an arena of learning, growth, and positive engagement! Grab your copy of this essential guide today and join countless satisfied readers who have effectively charted their course through the sea of social media interactions.

Chapter 2. Understanding the Land of Social Media

We initiate our expedition into this landscape by acknowledging the undeniable fact: social media isn't merely a facet of our lives, it's morphed into the very framework of our society, especially for today's younger generation. Mirroring the dynamic nature of human sociology, social media platforms today offer a kaleidoscope of interactive opportunities—each platform with its own quirks and characteristics.

2.1. Defining Social Media

Social media broadly encompasses web-based or mobile applications that enable individuals to create, share, or connect over user-generated content. Think of it as a digital gathering place that transcends the limitations of physical space and time. Within this digital realm, users can interact with each other in real-time or asynchronously, share an array of multimedia content—such as images, videos, and text—and cultivate virtual relationships far beyond their immediate vicinity. Key constituents include leading platforms like Facebook, Instagram, Twitter, Snapchat, and TikTok, alongside more niche offerings such as Pinterest, Clubhouse, and LinkedIn.

2.2. Evolution of Social Media: A Brief History

Social media wasn't woven into the societal fabric overnight. Let's trace back to its humble beginnings. The journey began with SixDegrees.com, launched in 1997, which allowed users to upload profiles and make friends. Subsequently, the advent of blogging and sites like MySpace and LinkedIn shaped the web's social structure. In 2004, the birth of Facebook took the world by storm, nowadays boasting over 2.8 billion monthly active users. Twitter's debut in 2006 introduced fresh dynamics with its microblogging system, while Instagram and Snapchat, launched in 2010 and 2011 respectively, heavily emphasized visual content. TikTok, a newer contender but extraordinarily popular, especially among young users, has become a cultural prodigy with its short-form, catchy videos.

2.3. Unravelling the Social Media Ecosystem

Dive headfirst into the social media ecosystem, with each application occupying a specialized niche, catering primarily to a specific user base, and offering a different mode of content sharing.

- Facebook stands as a virtual town square, encouraging sharing and active discussions on posts while simultaneously acting as an event planning hub and broadcast medium.

- Instagram is all about the visual canvas—photos, videos, and Stories—with influencers defining trends and shaping subcultures.

- Twitter capitalizes on real-time information exchange, ideal for news, debates, and live updates.

- Snapchat thrives on fleeting interactions with snaps that disappear after a single view, fostering a sense of momentary engagement.

- TikTok has raised the bar for creativity, with users creating short, addictive video clips set to various tunes.

2.4. Impact of Social Media on Society

Don't let the simplicity of these platforms fool you into undermining their impact. These platforms serve a much grander purpose than merely swapping pictures or chit-chatting. They are instrumental in how we consume news, form opinions, conduct business, express creativity, and build relationships.

Primarily, they have democratized information on an unprecedented scale. The colossal volumes of user-generated content yield a wide spectrum of perspectives on any topic under the sun. The result? An unparalleled potential for learning and personal development, and a shift from traditional, unidirectional knowledge sources to participatory, multidirectional ones.

However, social media can also be a double-edged sword. The advent of 'fake news,' private information breaches, cyberbullying, and screen addiction reflect the negative dimensions. These consequences call for robust digital literacy and cautious navigation of the social media landscape, themes we will address in the following chapters.

2.5. Our Responsibility in the Digital Landscape

Such a broad reach and profound impact naturally presuppose a significant responsibility. As we usher the younger generation into this digital landscape, it is incumbent upon us to ensure that they are well-equipped to reap the benefits of social media, while being vigilant of its potential pitfalls.

In this endeavour, understanding the terrain is the first step. Armed with this knowledge, one can better navigate the social media world, guide the young amongst us with confidence, and leverage these platforms' immense potential for progress, personal growth, and positive change.

Ultimately, like any tool, social media's impact largely depends on the wisdom and discretion with which it is used. The subsequent chapters of this guide will lead you through each aspect of this journey, ensuring that you're well-equipped to guide your teens through the intricate tapestry of their digital lives.

Chapter 3. The Digital Natives: How Teens Interact with Social Media

There is an undeniable truth hovering over our heads: we live in an era dominated by the Internet and digital technology. It's in this unprecedented context that today's teenagers – the so-called 'digital natives' – have grown up. Being part of a generation that knows no life without smartphones, tablets, and social media, they interact with these technologies in ways that often bewilder their 'digital immigrant' parents. This complex relationship with social media forms the heart of our exploration in this chapter.

3.1. The Digital Sphere: Understanding the Landscape

The virtual realm of social networks is like a second home for most teenagers. A report from the Pew Research Center found that 95% of teens in the U.S. have access to a smartphone, whilst 45% say they are online on a 'near-constant' basis. From consuming viral content on TikTok, expressing their creativity on Instagram, to connecting with friends on Snapchat, teenagers use social media as a tool for communication, collaboration, and community building.

A teenager's first interaction with social networks typically begins around age 12, coinciding with the start of middle school. At this point in their life, their world is expanding, and social media platforms provide an outlet for self-exploration and development. They use it to express their thoughts and showcase individuality, searching for their identity in the process. Employing hashtags, filters, TikTok challenges, or Instagram aesthetics, teens create virtual identities, taking complete liberty to experiment with their online persona.

This is not purely a solitary pursuit; social media platforms are rich with community-oriented engagement. Studies show that teens join various online communities based around shared interests, activities or causes - from promoting climate change activism, supporting LGBTQ+ rights, to fanbases for favored musicians or YouTubers. These digital interactions also serve to tackle the intricacies of social etiquette, helping young folks develop interpersonal skills.

3.2. The Consequences of Constant Connection

Teenagers' constant state of connection, though an extension of their social lives, comes with a set of challenges. Time spent on social media can lead to a dramatic decrease in physical activity and an increase in sedentary behavior. Teens are sacrificing sleep, homework, reading, and face-to-face interactions for the virtual social world.

Another consequence is the issue of "FOMO" or "Fear of Missing Out," a social anxiety exacerbated by social media. This syndrome is characterized by a desire to be continually connected with what others are doing, leading to compulsive checking of social media feeds and a constant feeling of inadequacy. Another aspect of this interaction comes from online comparisons with peers, adding another layer of pressure. The presentation of seemingly perfect bodies, lifestyles, and achievements can drive self-esteem issues among impressionable teens.

Further, social media can turn into a stage for cyberbullying, adding to the layers of interaction between teens and these platforms. Cyberbullying - the use of digital communication tools to make another person feel angry, sad, or scared, usually again and again - can lead to severe emotional trauma. This darker side of digital interaction enhances the complexities of navigating the world of social media for teenagers.

3.3. The Push and Pull: The Role of Social Validation

Among teenagers, there's a well-noted phenomenon of 'Like' culture. Teens chase after likes, comments, and shares as they seek validation from their peers, turning social media interactions into a quantifiable popularity contest. The role of dopamine, commonly known as the "feel-good hormone", is significant here. Every time teenagers receive a like or comment, dopamine is released, which fuels the desire for more engagement, thus creating a feedback loop. This fixation on seeking external validation can often overshadow the importance of self-worth and can lead to an unhealthy dependence on social media for self-esteem.

3.4. Digital Citizens: The Power and Responsibility

Like it or not, social media is instrumental in how teens shape and perceive the world around them. Embracing the power of technology, teens have used these platforms for positive change – mobilizing for climate change, campaigning for social justice, crowdfunding for charity, and amplifying silenced voices. Digital natives are therefore not just consumers; they are also creators and activists.

However, it is crucial to acknowledge the responsibilities that come with this power. The ability to comment, share, and post content publicly requires adherence to established norms and ethical guidelines. Teens need to understand the public nature of their digital footprints and maintain a conscientious and respectful online presence.

In conclusion, social media provides an intricate and multi-faceted platform for teenagers to interact, express themselves, and connect with the world. But like all powerful tools, it should be handled with care and respect. There is a unique language, power, and responsibility that comes with being digital natives, and comprehending this can help in fostering a positive and meaningful interaction with social media. It will inevitably continue to shape their social outlooks and encounters for years to come. Therefore, as their understanding of this continually evolving landscape deepens, it is vital they learn to navigate its opportunities and pitfall wisely.

Chapter 4. Social Media's Impact: The Good, The Bad, and the Ugly

In the rapid evolution of the digital world, social media has emerged as a dominant force shaping outlooks and influencing perspectives. From the way it weaves into the tapestry of adolescent daily life, social media's all-encompassing reach is apparent. Yet the repercussions are multifaceted, casting both constructive and malign shadows upon impressionable young minds. This chapter will take a deep dive into both the blessings and the curses of social media, meticulously unraveling the good, the bad, and the ugly.

4.1. The Good: Encouraging Connectivity and Learning Opportunities

It would be disingenuous to ignore the virtues of social media. The technique it has mastered, making our world a close-knit digital commune, is nothing short of remarkable. With just a click, young individuals can reach out to peers across the globe, breaking geographical barriers and cultivating a broadened worldview.

Social media also functions as an immensely valuable repository of knowledge. From exploring personal interests to gleaning complex academic concepts explained via engaging content, it has become an educational powerhouse. Online communities such as homework help forums, coding clubs, artist groups, and hobby societies shape enriching exchanges of ideas and knowledge. Such peer-learning opportunities can foster a more comprehensive understanding of different subjects, often far beyond the conventional classroom's scope.

4.2. The Bad: Heightened Exposure and Over-dependency

However, with every silver lining comes a cloud. Although appearing innocuous on the surface, the paradigm of constant connectivity can engender an unhealthy degree of dependency. Teens can find themselves tethered to their social media presence, with a significant chunk of their day consumed by incessant scrolling and refreshing feeds. The compulsion for digital validation – quantified through likes, shares, and comments – can create a dangerous spiral of over-dependency.

The enhanced exposure to the volatile matters of the world can also be counter-productive. The bombardment of information, new trends, and viral content can lead to information overload, culminating in mental fatigue or decision paralysis. Centering social life on the virtual platform may further engender virtual dysmorphia, significantly impacting self-perception and esteem.

4.3. The Ugly: Cyberbullying and Privacy Breaches

While social media can be a double-edged sword with potential benefits and drawbacks, there lies a dark underbelly too – the ugly facet. Vicious cyberbullying is a stark reality, with trolls targeting vulnerable teens, leaving profound psychological scars. The cloak of anonymity that certain platforms provide cultivates a hotbed of hostility and online violence.

Simultaneously, privacy breaches form another critical pitfall. With the net of surveillance growing ever-vigilant and personal information becoming a sought-after commodity, adolescents often inadvertently expose themselves to drastic repercussions. They might share sensitive information, negotiate their privacy or fall prey to scammers, hackers, and digital identity thieves.

Despite these concerns, it is essential to remember that social media is here to stay and evolve. Therefore, the onus is on us as parents, caregivers, educators, and society to guide our youth in conscientiously navigating their digital journey. Equipping them with digital literacy, critical thinking skills, self-respect, and respect for others will be key to harnessing social media's potential and minimizing its pitfalls.

In the following chapters, this book will delve into how to maintain a balanced interaction with social media, communicate effectively with teens about their digital presence, and empower them with digital literacy. It will further explore tackling cyberbullying and privacy concerns, leveraging social media for personal and academic growth, and empowering teens in today's social media era. By understanding the dynamics surrounding social media, we can walk hand-in-hand with our youth on their digital journey, ensuring a safer, more productive, and inspiring interaction with their connected world.

Chapter 5. Keys to a Healthy Digital Diet: Balance in Interaction

In an increasingly interconnected world where social media plays a pivotal role in how we communicate, it will come as no surprise that a 'digital diet', a term that refers to how we consume and interact with digital technology, is a concept of growing importance. Ensuring a balanced digital diet for teenagers is key to encouraging healthy online habits, demonstrably promoting positive interactions and effective learning.

5.1. Embracing a Balanced Approach

To promote a healthy interaction with social media platforms, we must first embrace a balanced approach. This approach comprises blended elements of time management, quality of interaction, and diversity of content. It aims to cultivate an environment where young individuals can reap the benefits of digital connections without letting them seep into every aspect of their lives. Our primary goal here should be quality, not quantity. Instead of being daunted by the amount of online content, teens should learn how to value the significance of meaningful exchanges.

5.2. Time Management and Social Media

Time management is a crucial facet of maintaining this balance. Our society tends to operate on a 24/7 basis due to the internet's constant accessibility, making it exceedingly easy to lose track of time when engaging with digital content. Therefore, incorporating time restrictions and breaks into teenagers' daily routines could arguably be the urgent necessity we must address. Scheduled 'digital detoxes', setting reasonable boundaries for the use of digital devices, and encouraging deliberate engagement with offline activities all contribute to healthier time management in a digital environment.

5.3. Interactions: Engaging Quality and Quantity

The type and quality of interactions on social media platforms dramatically influences our digital diet. With an abundance of opportunities to connect with peers and communities worldwide, it's essential to stress the quality of these interactions. Inculcating values of respect, patience, and empathy into online engagement, whether commenting on a friend's post or participating in a discussion on a forum, promotes positive online experiences and productive dialogues. This encourages a mindset where teenagers feel valued and heard—a liberating experience that fosters a better understanding of the diverse virtual world around them.

5.4. Diversity and Specified Content

A nutritious physical diet requires variety—this same principle applies to our digital diet. It is crucial to encourage teens to diversify their digital consumption, venturing beyond their immediate spheres of interest to discover fresh perspectives and broaden their knowledge and understanding. Allocating time to educational platforms and resources, exploring different cultures, or assessing different viewpoints on current events and trending topics, helps avoid the echo chamber effect and cultivates a more well-rounded digital experience.

5.5. Active and Passive Engagement

Engaging with social media is accomplished via two primary modes - active and passive. Active engagement involves posting, commenting, and actively participating in discussions, whereas passive engagement refers to consuming content without interaction, such as scrolling through feeds and reading posts. Both forms of engagement have their place in a balanced digital diet. The challenge is to create an equilibrium where active engagement and reflective passive engagement co-exist, creating a rich tapestry of experiential learning and growth.

5.6. Conclusion: Defining Your Digital Diet

In the final analysis, what constitutes a healthy digital diet is subjective and will differ based on individual interests, needs, and the uniqueness of their online interactions. However, maintaining balance, prioritizing quality interactions, managing time effectively, diversifying content, and understanding the role of active and passive engagement are universal ingredients for success. Encouraging teenagers to understand and implement these elements in their digital lives will foster an enriching online environment conducive to their personal, social, and cognitive development. Ultimately, the balanced digital diet is not just about combating the negatives, but harnessing and maximizing the positive potential of social media towards a balanced and fulfilling digital life.

Chapter 6. Bridging the Digital Gap: Communicating with Your Teen About Social Media

As we dive into the depths of this seminal chapter, it becomes abundantly clear that communication, as a pillar of all relationships, is paramount to bridging the digital gap between you and your teenager. This chapter aims to provide you with the knowledge, tools, and strategies necessary to navigate these seemingly treacherous but ultimately rewarding waters of digitally mediated communication.

6.1. Understanding the Digital Divide

In the context of modern society, the digital divide operates at multiple levels, from access to technological resources to the competency in using them. For parents, one of the most prominent aspects of this divide is the gap in understanding and usage of social media between them and their teens. The transformative power of social media platforms on the social, emotional, and cognitive development of today's teenagers cannot be overstressed. However, with this transformative potential comes a need to guide and navigate this uncharted territory. An understanding of their language, their tools, their pace, their challenges, and the values that govern them, is indispensable for you to bridge the divide effectively.

6.2. The Importance Of Open Dialogue

Initiating an open dialogue about social media with your teen is a crucial first step in bridging the digital gap. It's essential to move away from an adult-centric view and begin to see the digital world through their eyes. This entails discussions about their favorite platforms, what they find appealing about them, understanding their language, consuming the same content they do, and so forth. These conversations can often seem daunting for parents, but they go a long way in building trust and understanding, setting the stage for more serious discussions about privacy, safety, and responsible digital behavior.

6.3. Cultivating Trust and Understanding

Let us turn our focus to the mechanics of trust cultivation. It is essential to provide an environment where your teen feels comfortable discussing their online experiences, be it positive or negative. Your reactions to their narratives are likely to shape their willingness to share in the future. Instilling trust and understanding means resisting the urge to catastrophize, while also providing guidance to assure they are using social media platforms in a safe and responsible manner. Encourage their digital exploration, compliment their responsible online behavior, acknowledge their digital competency, and appreciate their effort to maintain a balanced digital life.

6.4. Developing Approachable Conversation Strategies

One effective strategy for conversations about social media with your teen is to use their consumption of digital content as a springboard for discussions. Instead of questioning their behavior, engage them in conversations about how they engage with that content—how it makes them feel, how it shapes their thoughts, if they agree with the viewpoints expressed, and so forth. This strategy not only allows you to gain a better understanding of their digital world but also provides an opportunity to inject positive values and critical thinking skills into their social media usage.

6.5. Explaining the Impact of Digital Footprints

A key part of bridging this digital gap involves educating your teen on the concept and implications of digital footprints. These are the trails of data left behind by their online activities. Ensuring they understand that whatever they share online, no matter how 'temporary' it may seem, leaves a footprint that could potentially be visible forever is essential. This understanding can empower them to make more responsible decisions when interacting on social media platforms.

6.6. Creating a Collaborative Atmosphere for Guided Digital Participation

Lastly, it is worth recognizing that you, the parents, also have a learning curve to scale. A collaborative atmosphere, where both you and your teen are learning from each other, can work wonders for bridging this gap. For example, if there is a new social media platform that your teen uses and that you are unfamiliar with, ask them to guide you through it. Such participatory digital activities boost their confidence while simultaneously allowing you to increase your digital literacy, resulting in a win-win situation for both parties.

To conclude, bridging the digital gap can be a challenging endeavor. However, with openness, understanding, guidance, and collaboration, it is undoubtedly a surmountable one. By adhering to the strategies and advice proposed in this chapter, you are surely headed in the right direction, fostering a relationship with your teen that is not torn apart by the digital divide but instead, bound closer due to it.

Remember, the objective is not to control but to guide and facilitate your teen's digital journey. The waters might seem murky at times, but with persistence, patience, and a compassionate hand at the helm, smoother sailing is undoubtedly on the horizon.

Chapter 7. The Invincible Armour: Building a Strong Digital Literacy

Building a robust digital literacy is akin to equipping oneself with an invincible armour in the world of social media. A digitally literate teen is not just competent in utilizing the tools and platforms provided by social media, but they also understand how to exploit these resources responsibly and safely.

7.1. The Edifice of Digital Literacy

The indispensable construction of digital literacy stands on three pillars: technological proficiency, critical understanding, and responsible engagement.

Technological proficiency is the first step towards digital literacy. It deals with familiarizing with the interfaces and operations of various social media platforms. This familiarity includes understanding the mechanics of posting, commenting, liking, sharing, blocking, reporting, etc., across numerous applications.

Critical understanding goes beyond technological proficiency and delves into the nuances of the information encountered on these platforms. It involves discerning reliable information from hoaxes, propaganda, or misinformation. It encapsulates privacy measures and how to respond to threats to one's digital wellbeing.

Responsible engagement, the last pillar, captures digital citizenship. It encompasses using these platforms ethically, responsibly, and with awareness of the potential consequences of online behaviours. This engagement includes recognizing one's role within digital communities and how one's interactions can impact others.

7.2. Importance of Building Digital Literacy

Digital literacy is crucial because it empowers youth to navigate the tumultuous seas of social media tools, platforms, and communities safely and effectively. It builds confidence in their online interactions and assists them in developing an informed perspective on the digital world. Moreover, digital literacy provides the protective shield necessary to tackle cyberbullying, safeguard oneself against digital dangers, and encourage a gratifying interactive experience.

7.3. Steps towards Building Robust Digital Literacy

Here are some steps that can help in building digital literacy:

1. Encourage Exploration: Allow your teen to explore different social media platforms under guidance. Familiarisation encourages understanding and adaptability.

2. Facilitate Learning: Guide your teen through different functionalities on each platform. Demonstrate how to report inappropriate content, block an intrusive user, customise privacy settings, etc.

3. Promote Critical Thinking: Encourage your teen to think critically about the information they encounter online. Teach them about the prevalence of fake news and how to distinguish between reliable and unreliable sources.

4. Discuss Ethics: Initiate conversations about online ethics. Stress upon the importance of respect in online communications, discourage spreading unverified information, and elaborate on the consequences of sharing inappropriate content.

5. Emphasise Digital Citizenship: Teach your teen about their part in

digital communities. Explain how their actions online can influence others and how they can contribute positively.

7.4. Employing Digital Literacy as a Guard

Strong digital literacy acts as a shield against online complications. It aids in recognising potential threats and malicious instances while teaching teens how to respond appropriately. It also cultivates an understanding that actions have repercussions, leading to more thoughtful communication and interaction.

7.5. Conclusion

In the age of social media where data is the new currency, and the digital persona is, at times, as important as the physical one, building a strong digital literacy is paramount. It assists our teens - the digital natives - not only to surf through the digital world with ease and confidence but also act responsibly and make informed choices. The protective layer of digital literacy enables them to stand strong against cyber menace and embrace the opportunities presented by the age of connectivity. It can indeed be their invincible armour in the social media-driven world.

Chapter 8. Tackling Cyberbullying: Strategies for Safety and Support

Cyberbullying is an unfortunate reality of the digital age, and this chapter delves into the lack and its harmful effects, setting forth proactive strategies to prevent it and to offer the necessary support when it occurs.

8.1. Understanding Cyberbullying

In the beginning, it's pivotal to understand what cyberbullying means. It captures everything from aggressive, intentional acts carried out by an individual or a group via digital devices to harm or intimidate others repeatedly. This modern form of bullying manifests through text messages, social media, apps, or online platforms that facilitate public communication and interaction. Cyberbullying takes on different forms, including sharing negative or false information about someone to damage their reputation, making derogatory comments, or forcing someone into undesirable online activities.

8.2. The Severity of the Problem

Assessing the severity of the problem is essential to realizing the significance of robust defensive actions against cyberbullying. Studies suggest that about 37% of young people between ages 12-17 have been bullied online and 30% have had it happen more than once. Cyberbullying can have traumatic psychological effects, leading to anxiety, depression, and, in severe cases, even suicide.

8.3. Identifying the Signs

Identifying signs of cyberbullying can be tricky as it often happens out of the adults' sight. Symptoms can include sudden withdrawal from technology or, conversely, an unusual increase in its use, exhibiting signs of emotional distress, especially after using the internet, a drop in school performance, or unexpectedly stopping to use social media platforms.

8.4. Educating About Cyberbullying

Education serves as the first line of defense against cyberbullying. Teens should be taught that anything that feels hurtful or uncomfortable is unacceptable online. This may include spreading rumors, name-calling, sharing explicit images, or threatening. They must be made aware of the long-lasting effects their actions can have on others and be encouraged to treat everyone with kindness and respect.

8.5. Empowering Teens to Handle Cyberbullying

Empowering teenagers to tackle cyberbullying independently is essential. They should feel competent to handle such situations by not replying or retaliating, blocking the bully, documenting evidence, and reporting the occurrence to trusted adults and if required, to social platforms or even the police.

8.6. Strategies for Parents and Caregivers

Parents can employ various strategies like being open to discussions about their teen's online experiences, taking their concerns seriously, clarifying the consequences of cyberbullying, and maintaining a channel of open communication. Also, parents must familiarize themselves with children's online activities and the platforms they frequent.

8.7. Implementing Tech-Based Solutions

Tech-based solutions like enabling privacy settings, managing friends' lists, and controlling who can see posts can be employed to prevent cyberbullying. In more severe cases, features like reporting abuse, blocking individuals, and making use of digital tools for tracking and controlling online activities can be helpful.

8.8. Supporting the Victim

If the teen falls victim to cyberbully, mental health support is crucial. Addressing the emotional trauma they face may require professional help. They shouldn't feel alone or blamed for the occurrence; it is important to reassure them it's not their fault.

8.9. Building Resilience

Building resilience to potential bullying situations is a significant aspect of handling cyberbullying. Help your teenager develop coping skills like dealing with stress, recognizing and managing emotions, understanding the difference between right and wrong, and building positive relationships offline.

This chapter underpins the seriousness of cyberbullying and the significant role parents play in preventing it and handling such situations effectively when they occur. As we move into an era characterized by digital interactions, creating an environment of respect and care in the online world is more important than ever. The next chapter will expand on 'Privacy Matters: Teaching Teens About Digital Footprints'.

Chapter 9. Privacy Matters: Teaching Teens About Digital Footprints

In the rapidly evolving terrain of digital technology, where impressions and expressions swivel in a fleeting second, the concept of 'Digital Footprint' becomes all the more significant. Defined as the trace or trail left behind as a result of one's online activity, digital footprints can be either passive or active. Passive digital footprints are created when data is collected about an action without the active contribution of the internet user, while active digital footprints are created when users intentionally share information on social media sites.

9.1. Understanding Digital Footprints

First and foremost, it's crucial to acknowledge the omnipresence of digital footprints. Imagine each online activity as a step taken in the digital sand; it leaves an indelible mark.

When we thread through the virtual world, whether it's a casual comment on a friend's photo, a like on a pop icon's video, an online purchase, or even a search for the nearest burger joint, we are doing so much more than mere interaction. We are populating the digital realm with information about us—our preferences, habits, dislikes, routines, and so much more.

In the age of algorithms, these footprints bristle with value as they shape our online experiences, tailor advertisements based on our preferences, and can even influence our decisions and future behaviors.

9.2. Risks Associated with Digital Footprints

While a digital footprint paints a vivid picture of our online persona, it also paves the way for potential risks and threats.

Online Privacy is one of the most significant concerns emerging from digital footprints. Every nugget of information shared or stored online can be susceptible to hacking and breaches. This violation can lead to identity theft, exposure to unwanted attention, or, worse, cyberstalking.

Reputation management is another aspect tangled with our digital footprints. Expressions shared impulsively can often alienate peers, harm relationships, or even impact opportunities. Employers, colleges, and scholarships often scout through social media during admissions or hiring to gain insights into what kind of person a candidate is. A single ill-advised post can turn the tide.

9.3. Educating Teens about their Digital Footprints

Imparting a wholesome understanding of digital footprints to teens is essential to equip them to navigate the online world responsibly.

1. Awareness: Start by educating them about the basics of digital footprints and how the internet etches every online movement.

2. Risk Assessment: Discuss the potential risks and implications tied to digital footprints.

3. Evaluation: Encourage them to assess their existing online presence and think critically about what it might tell others.

4. Privacy Settings: Discuss the importance of the privacy settings on different social networking sites and educate them on using

these effectively.

9.4. The Pathway to a Healthy Digital Footprint

As guiding forces in teens' lives, parents can facilitate the cultivation of a positive digital footprint.

Constant Dialogue: Keep the conversation about online safety and digital footprints ongoing. Discuss news related to cyber threats and how these situations could have been avoided.

Think Before You Post: Encourage them to follow the "THINK" strategy before posting: Is it True? Is it Helpful? Is it Inspiring? Is it Necessary? Is it Kind?

Positive Engagement: Encourage teens to share accomplishments, endorse causes they believe in, and connect with groups that reflect their interests. This active participation creates a positive online image.

In conclusion, our digital footprints are a reflection of who we are in this highly digitized world. If navigated wisely, they can serve as powerful tools for personal and professional growth. It's about time the motto 'Ignorance is Bliss' is replaced with 'Awareness is Power' in the conversation around digital footprints. Teach your teens about digital footprints and empower them to stride confidently into their digital future.

Chapter 10. Leveraging Social Media for Personal and Academic Growth

Leveraging social media for personal and academic growth involves understanding and exploiting the unique features of these digital platforms. In learning about such a productive relationship with social media, we delve into three significant focal points: Understanding the Role of Social Media in Personal Growth, Unraveling the Academic Potential of Social Media, and Implementing Balanced Social Media Use. Capitalizing on these three domains, we can then impart actionable skills and tools that will help teenagers shape their online presence into a beacon of growth and learning.

10.1. Understanding the Role of Social Media in Personal Growth

Social media is a powerful tool for honing and developing oneself—an arena to build networks, explore interests, and learn about different cultures and global events. Essentially, it has a profound influence on the development of a teenager's identity and worldview.

Self-expression is a key component of personal growth. Social media provides a wide variety of platforms where teenagers can express their thoughts, drive conversations around their interests, and shape their narrative in the digital world. Networking with like-minded individuals around the globe can bolster a teen's confidence, empathy, and global perspective. Consequently, it fosters cultural literacy and broadens their understanding of diverse worldviews.

Furthermore, social media can serve to amplify the voices of teenagers in societal discussions. By responsibly sharing and discussing societal issues, they get a firsthand experience of civic participation and a sense of community, which further bolsters their personal growth.

10.2. Unraveling the Academic Potential of Social Media

The academic implications of social media, although often overlooked, can offer an array of benefits. It offers educational resources that go beyond the confines of traditional textbooks, allowing teens to learn about various topics from quality, vetted sources.

Many educational institutions use social media platforms for sharing coursework, announcements, or supplemental resources. This can help students stay up to date with their academic work. Additionally, platforms such as YouTube and Pinterest provide an abundance of material that can assist in understanding complex topics. Videos, infographics, and illustrated guides can break down intricate concepts into easily digestible content.

Furthermore, social media promotes collaborative learning. Peer-to-peer interactions on these platforms can lead to discussions, debates, and joint problem-solving efforts. For instance, Facebook groups designed around academic subjects encourage students to communicate questions and provide peer feedback, contributing to a supportive learning environment.

Connecting with academic researchers, professors, and experts on platforms like Twitter or LinkedIn can encourage a passion for learning and expose students to the latest developments and discussions in their field of interest.

10.3. Implementing Balanced Social Media Use

While recognizing the benefits of social media is crucial, it's imperative that teens balance their online presence with their physical-world experiences. Setting boundaries for responsible social media use can ensure that it supplements, rather than overshadows, their personal and academic life.

Establishing a healthy social media diet involves setting time limits and taking regular digital breaks. This ensures that the majority of a teenager's time is not spent in front of a screen. Additionally, having broad-based interests outside of the digital realm can ensure well-rounded personal development.

Understanding that not everything one encounters on social media is accurate or useful is another key aspect of balanced use. Being selective about the sources of information consumed can mitigate the risks of misinformation and the adoption of extreme or polarized viewpoints. Encouraging fact-checking and critical thinking can enhance the educational potential of social media.

In conclusion, social media is an essential tool for teenagers in the digital age. It offers abundant possibilities for building networks, expressing oneself, and accessing educational resources. However, learning to implement balanced use of social media and ensuring the reliability of online information is equally important. With the right direction and guidance, social media can powerfully contribute to the personal and academic growth of today's teens.

Chapter 11. Moving Forward: Empowering Your Teen in the Age of Social Media

We live in a world where information is at our fingertips, educational resources are plentiful, and global collaboration is just a click away. Yet, as we weave forward through the intricate fabric of the digital revolution, it is essential to empower our teens with the necessary skills, strategies, and supportive environments that allow them to thrive.

11.1. The Importance of Digital Citizenship

The first step towards empowering our teens in the age of social media lies in the understanding and practice of good digital citizenship. Being a responsible digital citizen entails respecting oneself and others, staying safe online, and using the internet as a tool for learning and creativity, rather than merely consuming content. Encouraging teenagers to respect others' online spaces, think before they post, report inappropriate behavior, and understand the difference between fact and fake news are some substantial facets of digital citizenship. This is not a one-off lecture but continuous reinforcement and modeling of these behaviors can lead to better digital behavior.

11.2. Building Digital Resilience and Critical Thinking

Just as we build resilience in a physical environment, we need to empower teens with digital resilience as well. This means developing their ability to adapt and recover from issues they encounter online. Such problems might include a negative cyber interaction, a mistaken post that had unintended consequences, or possibly being hacked.

Equally crucial is fostering critical thinking. In this context, it refers to the ability to discern the reliability and credibility of the information they encounter online. Teaching your children to verify information from multiple trusted sources and be skeptical of one-sided arguments can go a long way. Regular family discussions about contemporary social media trends, news, and events can be an effective way to massage these critical thinking muscles.

11.3. Encouraging Personal Branding and Positive Digital Footprints

Each activity performed online leaves a digital footprint that, to some extent, forms an individual's online identity or personal brand. Encourage your teen to make conscious decisions about what they share online and how it can impact their future prospects, be it college admissions or job opportunities. Reinforce the idea that their online activities should reflect their passions, values, and aspirations. Their virtual self should be an extension of their real self.

A positive digital footprint can even be a boost to their career or college application. Emphasize on their sharing of creative works, participation in meaningful online communities, and their thoughtful commentary on societal issues.

11.4. A Supportive Digital Environment at Home

Setting clear household rules about social media use, monitoring online activities without breaching privacy, and openly talking about digital well-being can contribute to a supportive digital environment at home. A healthy routine, where teens have designated hours of unplugged time or social media breaks, can alleviate the risk of digital addiction. Periodically updating and upgrading digital security measures in all home devices are other small but significant steps towards a safer digital environment.

11.5. Fostering Healthy Online Relationships

Healthy relationships are just as critical online as they are offline. Conversations about the importance of respecting online relationships, empathetic digital communication, handling disagreements gracefully, and the perils of cyberbullying can help forge these healthy bonds. Introducing them to positive influencers in their areas of interest can assist them find meaningful connections, discover worthy role models, and cultivate effective networking skills.

In this digital era, social media and teens are inextricably linked. While the threads of this relationship can be complex, threading the needle in the right direction can empower them to make the most of their online engagement. Navigating the tumultuous tides of social media is not easy, but by fostering digital citizenship, resilience, critical thinking, personal branding, a supportive household environment, and healthy online relationships, we can empower our teens in the age of social media. It's time we turn this challenge into a beneficial opportunity, paving the way for confident, compassionate, and responsible digital citizens of the future.

www.ingramcontent.com/pod-product-compliance
Lightning Source LLC
Chambersburg PA
CBHW060858260726
48661CB00008B/3328